discover more
Life in a Community

Rules and Laws

Dwayne Hicks

Published in 2024 by Britannica Educational Publishing (a trademark of Encyclopædia Britannica, Inc.) in association with The Rosen Publishing Group, Inc.
2544 Clinton Street, Buffalo, NY 14224

Copyright © 2024 by Encyclopædia Britannica, Inc. Britannica, Encyclopædia Britannica, and the Thistle logo are registered trademarks Encyclopædia Britannica, Inc. All rights reserved.

Rosen Publishing materials copyright © 2024 The Rosen Publishing Group, Inc. All rights reserved.

Distributed exclusively by Rosen Publishing.
To see additional Britannica Educational Publishing titles, go to rosenpublishing.com.

All rights reserved. No part of this book may be reproduced in any form without permission in writing from the publisher, except by a reviewer.

Editor: Kathleen Klatte
Book Design: Leslie Taylor

Photo Credits: Cover Chinnapong/Shutterstock.com; (series background) Dai Yim/Shutterstock.com; p. 4 Marina N. Makarova/Shutterstock.com; p. 5 Federico Fermeglia/Shutterstock.com; pp. 6, 7 Michael O'Keene/Shutterstock.com; p. 9 (top) TR STOK/Shutterstock.com, (bottom) SpeedKingz/Shutterstock.com; p. 10 create jobs 51/Shutterstock.com; p. 11 Menna/Shutterstock.com; p. 12 Dima Moroz/Shutterstock.com; p. 13 Andrii Lutsyk/Shutterstock.com; p. 15 (top) Matthew Leigh/Shutterstock.com, (bottom) sirtravelalot/Shutterstock.com; p. 16 riopatuca/Shutterstock.com; p. 17 mark reinstein/Shutterstock.com; p. 18 Orhan Cam/Shutterstock.com; p. 19 Sean Pavone/Shutterstock.com; p. 20 MikeDotta/Shutterstock.com; p. 21 sirtravelalot/Shutterstock.com; p. 22 Elnur/Shutterstock.com; p. 23 bangoland/Shutterstock.com; p. 25 (top) Mary at T-Comms/Shutterstock.com, (bottom) Gorodenkoff/Shutterstock.com; p. 27 (top) JNix/Shutterstock.com, (bottom) Bob Korn/Shutterstock.com; p. 28 mark reinstein/Shutterstock.com; p. 29 Gabriele Maltinti/Shutterstock.com.

Cataloging-in-Publication Data

Names: Hicks, Dwayne.
Title: Rules and laws / Dwayne Hicks.
Description: New York : Britannica Educational Publishing, in Association with Rosen Educational Services. 2024. | Series: Discover more: life in a community | Includes glossary and index.
Identifiers: ISBN 9781642828849 (library bound) | ISBN 9781642828832 (pbk) | ISBN 9781642828856 (ebook)
Subjects: LCSH: Law--Juvenile literature. | Law--United States--Juvenile literature.
Classification: LCC K240.H53 2024 | DDC 340–dc23

Manufactured in the United States of America

Some of the images in this book illustrate individuals who are models. The depictions do not imply actual situations or events.

CPSIA Compliance Information: Batch #CSBRIT24. For further information contact Rosen Publishing at 1-800-237-9932.

Contents

Why Do We Need Rules?.............. 4

Rules for Every Kind of Community 6

Who's Responsible for All These Rules?.. 8

Rules Everyone Agrees On............. 10

Laws in Ancient Societies 12

Common and Civil Law.................14

Statute Law 16

Laws for Large Communities 18

Protecting the Community from Crime.. 20

Disagreements in the Community 22

The Legal Community 24

Changing with the Times 26

Laws in Your Community 28

Glossary 30

For More Information..................31

Index 32

Why Do We Need Rules?

Every community needs standards of behavior. These standards are called rules. Rules are everywhere: at home, at school, and wherever else people interact with each other. At home, parents set rules that teach children how to behave, such as not hitting your brother or sister. Rules at school can include raising your hand to talk and sitting in your seat until the teacher tells you to get up.

"Don't play ball in the house" is a very common rule. Why? Someone could get hurt on the broken glass. It will also cost money to repair the window.

Even adults follow the rules for an orderly fire drill. This helps keep everyone safe.

Though some rules can seem unnecessary at times, they are important. If everyone talked or moved around the class whenever they wanted, it would be hard for students to pay attention to the teacher and to learn.

Rules are not just for young people at home and in school. Everyone needs rules. That is why rules are a part of every kind of community. Laws are the official rules set down by government.

Consider This

Think about what would happen if people didn't obey traffic rules and stop at red lights or crosswalks. The community wouldn't be very safe, would it?

Rules for Every Kind of Community

A group of people who occupy the same place and use the same resources is called a community. People usually belong to more than one community. For instance, a neighborhood is one kind of community and a school is another kind. There are even online communities where people talk or play games. All of these communities need rules so that the communities continue to work well and support people's interests and goals.

Speed limits are rules for drivers. They need to drive slowly where people might be walking or riding bikes.

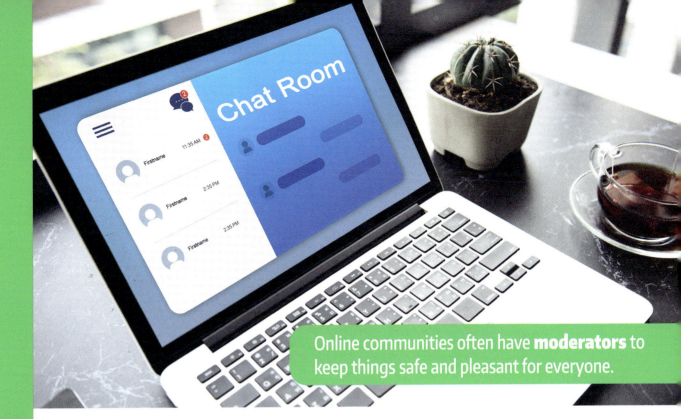

Online communities often have **moderators** to keep things safe and pleasant for everyone.

Communities in which people live, from small villages to large countries, have governments that make rules requiring or prohibiting certain actions. These rules are called laws. Laws keep the community safe and orderly for the people who live there.

WORD WISE

A moderator is someone who helps run an online community. They might remind people to stick to the group's topic or not use bad language. They can also ban people who post unsafe content to the group.

Who's Responsible for All These Rules?

Community leaders make laws and rules that are appropriate for the type of community and the people who occupy it. Some cities have zoning laws that say noisy or smelly factories cannot be built in certain zones, or areas, where people live. There may be laws and rules in special parts of communities, too. For example, in order to keep people safe after dark, visitors often need to leave city or state parks by sunset.

People have a responsibility to the other members of their community to follow laws that keep the community working well. Also, there are consequences for not following laws. Many communities have organizations for enforcing laws and keeping order. The most common type of law enforcement agency is a police force.

Yuck! Who wants to breathe that? The Environmental Protection Agency (EPA) is a federal agency. They make rules about pollution.

compare and contrast

Why are rules about pollution made by a federal agency? Why are health and traffic laws made locally?

A health department is usually a local agency. They make rules about keeping public places clean and serving food safely.

Rules Everyone Agrees On

There are some actions that all people agree are wrong. These are called natural laws. Stealing and killing are both forbidden by natural law. These natural laws are translated into community laws throughout the world.

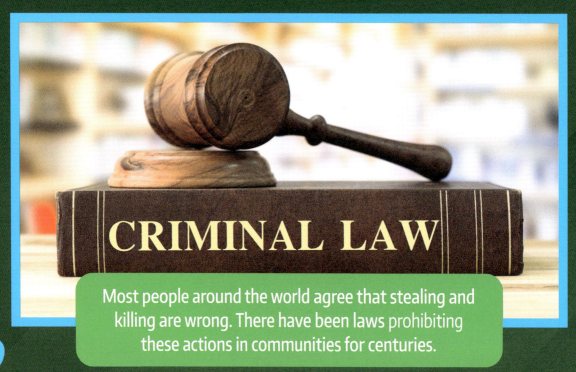

Most people around the world agree that stealing and killing are wrong. There have been laws prohibiting these actions in communities for centuries.

Building codes are positive laws.

Law that is based on rules created by rulers or lawmakers is called positive law. Speed limits on roads are positive laws. Most natural laws have become adopted as positive laws.

Lawmaking bodies of government called legislatures make laws. Laws can change over time. Sometimes people decide that old ideas don't work well in their community anymore.

Consider This

Most people agree that killing and stealing are wrong. However, there are many different ideas about suitable punishments for these crimes. Why do you think that is?

Laws in Ancient Societies

As long as humans have lived in communities, they've needed systems of rules and laws. One of the best known of the early codes, or collections of written laws, is that of Hammurabi. He was a king of Babylon who lived almost three thousand years ago. Probably the most famous of the ancient codes is the Ten Commandments. The commandments are a basic summary of moral laws followed by members of several different religions.

The Code of Hammurabi still exists. It's on display at the Louvre Museum in Paris, France.

The emperor Justinian is remembered for his compilation of Roman law, the *Corpus Juris Civilis.*

All other societies in the ancient world created sets of laws. In the democracy of ancient Athens in Greece, the citizens agreed on the laws that would govern them. Some modern governments are based on these ancient democratic principles.

Consider This

Many ancient legal codes called for harsh punishments, including death, for many crimes. Today's laws are often based on the idea of helping criminals become productive members of the community after they've paid a fine or spent time in prison.

Common and Civil Law

Two of the main systems of law used today are common law and civil law. Common law developed in England hundreds of years ago. Judges make decisions about cases based on decisions in earlier cases. British settlers brought common law with them to the North American colonies of England that became the United States.

In Europe and Latin America, many countries base their laws on the civil code. In 1804, French emperor Napoleon I introduced this wide-reaching system of laws. It was meant to break free from past laws that were unfair to certain groups of people. Judges relying on the Napoleonic civil code use the laws instead of past judgments to make decisions.

An amended form of Napoleon's civil code is still used in France today.

compareandcontrast
Which do you think is more fair, common law or civil law?

Common law judges have to be familiar with many previous legal decisions, called precedents.

Statute Law

Another system of law is called statute law. A statute law is made by a legislature. In the United States, Congress passes federal laws in Washington, D.C. Each state also has its own legislature that makes statute laws strictly for that state. Statute laws are made in local lawmaking bodies in smaller communities as well, such as in city councils and town councils.

The Americans with Disabilities Act of 1990 (ADA) is a federal statute. It says that employers can't discriminate against disabled people. It also says that all public places must be accessible to disabled people.

The ADA was signed into law by President George H.W. Bush in 1990.

Statute laws developed because common law does not apply in all cases. Sometimes statute laws deal with situations that are so new that a judge cannot look at decisions from earlier cases. Statute laws can also be a way to make the decisions from common law official. Important federal statutes can also be called acts.

Consider This

The ADA is a statute law that makes life safer and easier for disabled community members. Ramps, automatic doors, and bathrooms with safety bars also benefit other members of the community, such as the elderly.

Laws for Large Communities

The most important law in the United States is the U.S. Constitution. It describes the branches of the government and their separate powers. The Constitution also gives the federal, or national, government the power to make certain laws. Federal laws apply to everyone in the whole country. These laws include regulations about **immigration**, federal crimes (such as not paying your taxes), and many other things.

Congress is the lawmaking body of the federal government. Members of Congress meet at the U.S. Capitol Building in Washington, D.C.

Albany is home to the New York State Capitol. Do you know your state's capital? It's not always the biggest or most famous city in the state.

The Constitution makes sure that each state has the power to make laws that must be obeyed within that state. Laws may be different from state to state. State laws deal with crime, businesses, family law, and even how long a student must attend school.

Other large countries, like Canada, have similar systems. Some countries are so small that they don't need state governments.

WORD WISE

Immigration is the act of moving from one country to another to live and work.

Protecting the Community from Crime

Most laws fall into one of two categories: criminal or civil. Criminal law deals with crime, which occurs when a person breaks a law. Crimes are harmful to communities. They include such acts as murder, robbery, and assault. They also include offenses that may seem harmless, such as driving through a stop sign, but that could result in injury or death. The government usually puts people accused of breaking laws on trial in a court.

Directing traffic is one way local police officers help keep your community safe.

When someone is accused of a crime, their trial is decided by a jury—a group of people randomly selected from the community.

If the court finds the accused—called the defendant—guilty, he or she is punished. Punishments depend on the seriousness of the crime. Less serious crimes such as shoplifting may be punished with a fine or community service. More serious crimes result in a prison term or even death, depending on the state.

In a criminal case, the government of the community whose law was broken brings charges against the person accused of breaking the law.

Consider This

Why do you think it's important for a jury to decide if someone is guilty or innocent, instead of a judge?

Disagreements in the Community

A civil case is a disagreement between two people or groups. A person or group, also called a party, files a lawsuit in a civil court if they think another party has treated them unfairly. The party who files the suit is called the plaintiff. Usually the plaintiff wants money or a change in conduct from the opponent, called the defendant.

A divorce is a type of civil case. It's a disagreement between two individuals.

Disagreements between tenants and landlords are civil cases. They might be between two individuals or between an individual and a company.

If the court agrees with the plaintiff, it will issue either an injunction or monetary damages against the defendant. An injunction is an order that the defendant must take some action. For example, the defendant might have to deliver goods that were promised to the plaintiff in a contract. Civil cases might involve money, property damage, or a breach of contract.

Consider This

A person who's accused of a crime may face both criminal and civil charges. The government will press charges for the law they broke. The victim (or their family) may file a civil suit for things like property damage or medical bills.

The Legal Community

A courthouse is like a small community. The official in charge of each court is a judge. He or she hears the different sides of each case and makes decisions about the law. Judges often oversee a jury.

There are several different levels of courts within the United States. For example, breaking a state law requires a person to appear in a state court. If a defendant loses a case, he or she may challenge, or appeal, the decision in a higher court. Eventually a case may reach the Supreme Court, the highest court in the country.

The legal system is very complex. People who go to school to study the law are called lawyers or attorneys. Lawyers represent both sides in a civil or criminal case.

Law school graduates have to pass the bar exam before they can practice.

compare and contrast
Which job do you think is more important, defense attorney or prosecutor?

Judges can be elected or appointed. They also need to possess a law degree.

Changing with the Times

The way people live and think is always changing. Laws are added or changed to address new problems. Consider how much technology has transformed the world. In many U.S. states and all Canadian provinces, there are now laws against holding a cell phone while driving. These laws are meant to protect people from distracted driving.

Sometimes people realize that old ideas are unfair. They demand that laws change to correct injustices. An amendment to the U.S. Constitution finally gave women the right to vote in 1920. In 1990 the Americans with Disabilities Act guaranteed that people with physical or mental disabilities would have equal opportunities in their jobs, in schools, and in public places.

The Montgomery Bus Boycott protested the community's unfair treatment of African Americans.

compareandcontrast

Generally, nonviolent protests are more likely to have good results. Other times, protests can become violent or disruptive. Which way do you think is better for the community?

When people want to change a law that affects the whole country, they often protest in Washington, D.C.

Laws in Your Community

Every community—large or small—has laws. Not everyone agrees with all of them. Some people think there are too many laws and that the government should not be so involved in people's lives. For example, some people think there should be fewer laws about drugs. Others disagree with communities that outlaw foods that are bad for people's health. On the other hand, many citizens think more laws will keep communities safer and healthier.

A hearing is a public meeting where community members can discuss issues that affect them, such as proposals for new laws.

Most communities have laws against parking in front of fire hydrants. This helps keep everyone in the community safe.

People need to be active and informed about their community's laws. They should keep up to date about existing laws and about possible future laws that the government is considering. Everyone in a community can have a say about the laws in that community. You might not be old enough to vote yet, but you can learn about your community's issues and even communicate with its leaders.

Consider This

Ask your parents about the leaders they vote for. Why do they think they're good for your community?

Glossary

amendment: A change in the words or meaning of a law or document, such as a constitution.

ancient: Of, coming from, or belonging to a time that was long ago in the past.

assault: An unlawful attempt or act of harm toward a person.

civil code: A set of rules that define the law without relying on past judgements.

complex: Having many parts, details, or ideas that can be hard to understand.

consequence: A result or effect.

contract: A legally binding agreement between two or more parties.

disability: A condition (such as an illness or an injury) that damages or limits a person's physical or mental abilities.

disrupt: To throw into disorder.

distracted: Drawing the attention or mind to something else.

enforcing: Carrying out or bringing about, sometimes by force.

immigration: The act of going to another country in order to live there.

legislature: An organized body of persons having the authority to make laws.

moral: Having to do with the judgment of right or wrong in human behavior.

prohibiting: Not allowing.

province: A large division of a country having its own government.

regulation: A rule or order telling how something is to be done.

responsibility: A duty or requirement.

summary: A short statement of main points.

technology: The use of science in solving problems.

For More Information

Books

Bush, Zack, and Laurie Friedman. *The Little Book of the Supreme Court.* Publishing Power, LLC, 2022.

Pittman, Portia, and Dr. Calvin Mercer. *There Ought to Be a Law: A Bright Day at the State Capitol.* Bright Books, 2020.

Websites

The Judicial System
www.ducksters.com/history/us_judicial_branch.php
Ducksters has a page about the judicial branch of the U.S. government. It includes a quiz.

U.S. Supreme Court
www.supremecourt.gov/visiting/activities.aspx
The official website of the U.S. Supreme Court has lots of fun age-appropriate activities for kids and families.

Publisher's note to educators and parents: Our editors have carefully reviewed these websites to ensure that they are suitable for students. Many websites change frequently, however, and we cannot guarantee that a site's future contents will continue to meet our high standards of quality and educational value. Be advised that students should be closely supervised whenever they access the internet.

Index

A
Athens, Greece, 13

C
civil case, 22, 23, 24
civil law, 14, 15, 20
Code of Hammurabi, 12
common law, 14, 15, 17
Corpus Juris Civilis, 13
criminal case, 20, 23, 24

H
health department, 9
home, 4, 5

L
legislatures, 11, 16

N
Napoleonic civil code, 14, 15
natural laws, 10, 11

O
online community, 7

P
police, 8, 20
positive laws, 11
punishment, 13, 21

S
school, 4, 5, 6
statute law, 16, 17
Supreme Court, 24

T
Ten Commandments, 12
traffic rules, 5, 6, 9, 20

U
U.S. Constitution, 18, 19

Z
zoning laws, 8